READ. RUMINATE. REFLECT.

Todd D. Ca

Reflection
of the
SON

Todd Coburn

WESTBOW
PRESS®
A DIVISION OF THOMAS NELSON
& ZONDERVAN

Unless otherwise noted, all Scripture quotations are taken from the Holy
Bible, New International Version. Copyright © 1973, 1978, 1984, 2011.

WestBow Press books may be ordered through booksellers or by contacting:

WestBow Press
A Division of Thomas Nelson & Zondervan
1663 Liberty Drive
Bloomington, IN 47403
www.westbowpress.com
1 (866) 928-1240

Because of the dynamic nature of the Internet, any web addresses or
links contained in this book may have changed since publication and
may no longer be valid. The views expressed in this work are solely those
of the author and do not necessarily reflect the views of the publisher,
and the publisher hereby disclaims any responsibility for them.

Any people depicted in stock imagery provided by Thinkstock are
models, and such images are being used for illustrative purposes only.
Certain stock imagery © Thinkstock.

Cover Photo: *Martian Moonrise*

Original Photograph by Wally Pacholka

This picture of the moon as it rises through Arch Rock in The Valley
of Fire State Park in Nevada was generously provided as cover art for
this book by Wally Pacholka, who reserves all rights and the copyright
for this photo. Additional amazing photos are available directly
from Wally through his website http://www.astropics.com/.

ISBN: 978-1-5127-3136-1 (sc)
ISBN: 978-1-5127-3137-8 (e)

Library of Congress Control Number: 2016902487

Printed in the USA

WestBow Press rev. date: 03/02/2016

Contents

This book is dedicated...

to my parents,

Franklin & Kitti Coburn

and to my grandparents

Frank & Marjorie Coburn

four magnificent reflections

of the

Son

May I emulate Christ as well as they someday.

Preface

Dear Reader,

Have you ever had one of those moments when you experienced something in life that triggered an understanding of something else at a deeper level than you had previously suspected? Often these two items are unrelated, yet the one exhibits some parallel behavior or pattern that sheds light on the inner workings of something totally different. Having recognized and understood this deeper truth, your mind races forward, connecting this and other things and understanding them in a way that you had only vaguely understood prior to your epiphany.

I had one of those moments not long ago, when I believe God used a simple process of nature to awaken me from my daily routine so that He could reveal truths about Himself that provided staggering insights into my roles and responsibilities as a Christian.

I suspect that what God revealed to me could also be of benefit to you, and to all those who wish to be better reflections of Jesus Christ to our neighbors around us, and to the world.

In this book I have recorded some of the revelations and insights that have resulted from that first epiphany in this area, and I hope you find these insights as exciting and useful in your daily walk as I have.

My prayer is that the Lord bless you as you read this book by confirming through His Spirit the truths that He wishes to set in your heart, and by shaping these truths into life-changing actions that enable you to better reflect His Word, His Will and His Ways to all mankind.

Your brother in our Lord Jesus Christ,
Todd Coburn

1

Moon Model

Imagine stepping outside in the wee hours of the morning. The air is clear and crisp and the cold nibbles at your skin through your freshly pressed shirt. It is dark out, but not too dark. The air is really more of a blue hue, and the plants and trees cast dark blue-black shadows across the cobblestones under your heel. You raise your eyes to find the source of the shadows in that pale blue light, and your eyes widen to find the huge silver-white orb of the moon, hanging low and full just above the horizon. Stars surround the moon, like the tiny points of light from pinholes in a sheet of paper held up to the light. You catch your breath, motionless at the beauty and perfection of that silver light piecing the darkness.

As you stand admiring the beauty of the effects of the moon's light on the terrain, you suddenly realize that the moon has no light of its own, and that this wonderland of beauty isn't caused by the light of the moon at all, but by the light of the sun reflecting off of the surface of the moon from far beyond your vision. The thought strikes that this breathtaking display is made possible by the moon being positioned precisely so that its full face is able to reflect the light of the sun. The result of this miraculous coupling of moon positioning with sun radiance is blue light radiating into each crevice of a darkened portion of the earth.

That's when you realize that half the world at that moment stands in darkness, impenetrable darkness devoid of the light of the sun. Yet because of the moon's careful positioning, these people who would otherwise be in utter darkness are able to see dimly. They are able to see due to the reflection of the sun off of the surface of the moon.

This simple fact of nature provides staggering insight into the role of a Christian in this fallen world. The God of this world has chosen to provide light to all mankind through His Son, who was crucified and died so that we could be cleansed and made free. For a time the light of Jesus shone directly on this earth, testifying to God's grace and love, and demonstrating the kind of life God desires from those who love and serve Him. Yet in the same way that Jesus reflected God's light into the world when He was here, God has chosen that we now reflect Jesus' light into this fallen world until He returns. We will explore this further in coming chapters.

2

Lunar Lesson

We saw in the last chapter how the moon provides light to the darkened portion of the world. It does so by reflecting the light of the sun. We were reminded that the moon has no light of its own, but simply reflects the light of the sun to the earth. If one day the moon chose not to reflect the sun's light, but instead hid itself from the sun's face and tried to shine its own light to the earth, it would fail miserably. Those standing in darkness and looking to the sky for light would find only deeper blackness emanating from the moon itself.

We could conclude that in order for the moon to provide light to the darkened world, it must (1) understand that the sun is the source of light, (2) understand that the moon has no light of its own, (3) understand that only by reflecting the sun's light can the moon help illuminate the earth, and (4) position itself so that it faces the sun, so that the sun can reflect its light off the moon's face.

This simple formula is the key to the moon's success for lighting a dark night. It is also an incredibly simple model that a Christian can use to shine the light of the Son, Jesus Christ, to a spiritually darkened world.

We can conclude that in order for a Christian to provide light to a spiritually darkened world, he must (1) understand that the Son, Jesus Christ, is the source of all spiritual light, (2) understand that he (the Christian) has no light of his own, (3) understand that only by reflecting the Son's light can the Christian help illuminate the earth with the knowledge of Jesus Christ, and (4) position himself so that he faces the Son, so that Jesus Christ can reflect His light off of the Christian's face and through the Christian's actions, character, and behavior.

We will explore each of these principles in the following chapters.

3

Son Source

If our goal as Christians is to do our part in shedding as much light onto the earth as possible, then it is critical that we understand the source of light. Scripture reveals that the first principle for the Christian to follow in his quest to become a light to the world is to understand that the Son, Jesus Christ, is the source of all spiritual light. Let's explore a few of the key passages of Scripture that lay the foundation for this principle.

Jesus, the Word, is the Source of Creation, Life, and Light (John 1:1-5)

The Gospel of John starts with an incredibly simple truth. John 1:1+ reads as follows.

> ¹*In the beginning was the Word, and the Word was with God, and the Word was God.*

> *²He was with God in the beginning. ³Through him all things were made; without him nothing was made that has been made. ⁴In him was life, and that life was the light of all mankind. ⁵The light shines in the darkness, and the darkness has not overcome it.*

This statement is simple, direct, and profound. It identifies and reveals a being called "The Word" who was in the beginning with God, and who in actual fact was God. It presents this "Word" as present <u>with</u> God, as part <u>of</u> God and yet as separate <u>from</u> God. It identifies this "Word" as participating in creation, which again identifies Him with God, since we know from Genesis and elsewhere that <u>God</u> created everything. Yet we find here that all things were made <u>through</u> Him (the Word). This statement that all things were made <u>through</u> Him reveals that the Word did not create all things alone (on His own), but that he <u>participated</u> in creation, since all creation occurred not merely <u>by</u> Him but especially <u>through</u> Him.

This passage goes on to state that <u>in</u> this Word was life. This means that the Word has life <u>within</u> Himself, not only <u>for</u> and <u>of</u> Himself, but also <u>available for others</u>. This simple statement identifies the Word as the

<u>source</u> of life. This truth is in perfect agreement with the whole of Scripture (See also Matthew 19:29, Mark 10:30, John 3:15-16, 3:36, 4:14, 5:21, 5:24-29, 5:39-40, 6:27-40, 6:47-58, 8:12, 10:28, 11:25, 14:6, 17:2-3, 20:31, Acts 3:15, Rom 5:21, 6:23, I Tim 1:16, 2 Tim 1:1, 1:10, I John 1:1-2, 5:11-13, 5:20).

The passage continues and reveals that this life within and available from the Word is also the light of all mankind. Since the Word is the source of life, and this life is light, we find here that the Word is the source of light for all mankind. This light enables mankind to see. It provides the environment and the energy so we can live. This life from the Word is light, and this light is life, and the Word is the source of it (See also Matt 4:16, John 1:7, 1:9, 3:19, 8:12, 9:5, 12:46).

The passage continues by revealing that the light shines in the darkness and that the darkness has not overcome it. This statement is also simple and profound. It reveals that there is light and there is darkness. The Word is the source of light, and He shines in the darkness. Since He is the source of light, we can conclude that there is no light apart from Him. This means that without this Word mankind is destined to darkness. Since the light is life, those who live in darkness will have neither light nor life. What a bleak existence mankind faces without the Word to provide light and life! Fortunately for us the light shines in the darkness.

We also see here that there is a struggle going on, a conflict of light versus darkness. The Word is the source of light, and this light is shining in the darkness, and the darkness is fighting to snuff out that light, yet it cannot.

This simple passage in verses 1-5 of the Gospel of John lays the structure of the Gospel. The Word is God. He is with God, part of God, and yet separate from God. His action (at least in creation) is inclusively with, part of, and separate from God. He is the source of life, and of light, and He is the light of mankind. His light shines in the darkness and although the darkness wishes to overcome His light it has not been able to do so.

Those familiar with Scripture can glean from these verses who this "Word" is, but for those less familiar with Scripture, the Spirit reveals Him through the apostle John a few verses later in John 1:14, as follows:

> *14The Word became flesh and made his dwelling among us. We have seen his glory,*

> *the glory of the one and only Son, who came*
> *from the Father, full of grace and truth.*

The Word is the One who became flesh, the One who dwelt among us, the glorious Son of God who came from God the Father. The Word is Jesus Christ.

This is clarified further in verse 15 to 18.

> *[15](John testified concerning him. He cried out, saying, "This is the one I spoke about when I said, 'He who comes after me has surpassed me because he was before me.'")*
> *[16]Out of his fullness we have all received grace in place of grace already given. [17]For the law was given through Moses; grace and truth came through Jesus Christ. [18]No one has ever seen God, but the one and only Son, who is himself God and is in closest relationship with the Father, has made him known.*

Jesus is the one who brings us grace and truth. Jesus is Himself God, and Jesus makes God known to us.

Verses 29-34 make it even clearer that Jesus is the Word who this passage is making known.

²⁹The next day John saw Jesus coming toward him and said, "Look, the Lamb of God, who takes away the sin of the world! ³⁰This is the one I meant when I said, 'A man who comes after me has surpassed me because he was before me.' ³¹I myself did not know him, but the reason I came baptizing with water was that he might be revealed to Israel." ³²Then John gave this testimony: "I saw the Spirit come down from heaven as a dove and remain on him. ³³And I myself did not know him, but the one who sent me to baptize with water told me, 'The man on whom you see the Spirit come down and remain is the one who will baptize with the Holy Spirit.' ³⁴I have seen and I testify that this is God's Chosen One."

Jesus Christ is God's Chosen One. He will baptize mankind with the Holy Spirit. Jesus is the Word. He is with God. He is God. He is both part of and yet separate from God. He is the source of life and light. He is the light of mankind. No one who believes in Him need stay in darkness. He is the source of creation.

These passages make clear that Jesus is the source of life, light, and creation. Yet Jesus is the source of even more than that. We will investigate this further in the following sections.

Jesus is the Source of Our Inheritance, the Kingdom of Light (Colossians 1:9-14)

Jesus is not only the source of light, He is also the source of our inheritance in His Kingdom of Light. The Holy Spirit reveals this truth through the apostle Paul in the book of Colossians. His thoughts on the subject begin in the middle of verse 9 of the first chapter, as follows:

> *[9b]We continually ask God to fill you with the knowledge of his will through all the wisdom and understanding that the Spirit gives [10]so that you may live a life worthy of the Lord and please him in every way: bearing fruit in every good work, growing in the knowledge of God, [11]being strengthened with all power according to his glorious might so that you may have great endurance and patience, [12]and giving joyful thanks to the Father, who has qualified you to share in the inheritance of his holy people in the kingdom of light. [13]For he has rescued us from the dominion of*

> *darkness and brought us into the kingdom
> of the Son he loves, [14]in whom we have
> redemption, the forgiveness of sins.*

This passage is a prayer of Paul for the Christians in Colossae. It is written to and for the Christians in Colossae, and yet it reveals a truth that is universal for all Christians. When Paul says "you" in this passage he is referring to the Christians in Colossae, and since he is describing their position as Christians we can see that this truth also applies to all Christians in general. When he says "us" in the passage he is referring to the Christians in Colossae, and himself, and all others who are also Christians, so we can see that this also applies universally to all Christians. Therefore we see that while the apostle Paul is writing to the Christians in Colossae, the Holy Spirit is revealing through him a number of truths that are foundational for every believer. Let's take a look at them in order.

In verse 12 we see that God the Father has qualified us (Christians) to share in the inheritance of His holy people in the kingdom of light. The statement that He qualified us means that we were not qualified, but that through some action on God the Father's part He has qualified us, or made it possible for us. The thing

He has qualified us for is to share in an inheritance with His holy people. An inheritance is something given to us that is unmerited or undeserved. An inheritance is usually given to a child, or to a relative, or to a dear friend. It is usually given to someone due to a relationship that is being honored. It is sometimes selfishly and erroneously claimed as something due by would-be relatives or friends, but it is more generally and accurately recognized as an action of grace on the part of the one giving the inheritance towards the person or persons receiving the inheritance. We are sharing this inheritance with God's holy people, which refers to all those whom God has set apart and made holy and qualified to share in this inheritance. We see that this inheritance we share in is membership in the kingdom of light.

In verse 13 we see that God the Father has rescued us from the dominion of darkness and brought us into the kingdom of the Son he loves. From this we see that the kingdom of light that we have been qualified to share in due to our inheritance from God the Father is really the kingdom of the Son He loves, Jesus Christ. We also see that before being qualified to share in this kingdom we were under the dominion of darkness. Yet since He chose to qualify us to be rescued we have escaped that dominion of darkness and we now share in the kingdom of light.

In verse 14 we see that due to this inheritance in Jesus' kingdom of light, we have through Jesus redemption, which is the forgiveness of sins.

This passage in Colossians is in perfect agreement with the passage in John. The two passages present parallel truths that perfectly agree and complement each other such that each provides insight into some facet of the other.

In John 1 we saw that the Word (Jesus) is the light of the world and of all mankind. This light (Jesus) shines in the darkness and the darkness has not overcome it. Whoever follows Jesus will never walk in darkness, but will have the light of life. No one who believes in Jesus will stay in darkness.

In Colossians 1 we see that all mankind is trapped under the dominion of darkness, but that God has rescued some by qualifying them to receive the inheritance of membership in the kingdom of light, which is the kingdom of His Son, Jesus Christ. In Jesus we also have redemption, the forgiveness of sins.

When we look at John we see that those who believe in Jesus and who follow Him will not stay in darkness, but will have the light of life. When we look at Colossians we see that all mankind is trapped under the dominion of darkness except those who are rescued by God and qualified to share in Jesus' kingdom of light. When we look at these passages together we see that the way to be rescued by God and to be qualified to share in Jesus' kingdom of light is by believing in Jesus and by following him.

In John we see that in Jesus is life, and this life is the light of mankind. We also see that life and light are synonymous in Jesus. In Colossians we see that Jesus has a kingdom of light, and that in Him we have redemption, the forgiveness of sins. When we examine these passages together we recognize that Jesus' kingdom of light is also a kingdom of life. We see that rescue and redemption and the forgiveness of sins are all intertwined and made possible in Jesus.

These truths are beautiful to behold. Turning these truths over in our minds can be like examining diamonds or precious jewels in the palms of our hands. As we turn them round and round in our fingers, and examine each of their many facets, we see more and more beauty in the cut and shape and depth of these truths. Yet there is more. At this point in Colossians the Holy Spirit in Paul is just beginning to come to the most beautiful and deep of His truths about the nature and role of this Jesus Christ, the Son of God, who has a name and a nature that redefines our human concepts of Word and light and life.

Jesus is God, the Source of all things (Colossians 1:15-20)

Let's take a deep breath and look further at what the Holy Spirit reveals in Colossians chapter one verse 15 and following.

> *[15]The Son is the image of the invisible God, the firstborn over all creation. [16]For in him all things were created: things in heaven and on earth, visible and invisible, whether thrones or powers or rulers or authorities; all things have been created through him and for him. [17]He is before all things, and in him all things hold together. [18]And he is the head of the body, the church; he is the beginning and the firstborn from among the dead, so that in everything he might*

> *have the supremacy. ¹⁹For God was pleased to have all his fullness dwell in him, ²⁰and through him to reconcile to himself all things, whether things on earth or things in heaven, by making peace through his blood, shed on the cross.*

Wow. Isn't this beautiful? Every time I read this passage my heart takes a leap and mentally I plant my knees and forehead in the dust, raise my arms in the air, and in my heart shout praises to Jesus Christ, the Son of God who is also fully and completely God.

What a profound truth! This passage is one of many that provide inescapable clarity to the fact that Jesus Christ is fully and completely God. Let's examine each facet of this exquisite gem of truth from Colossians.

In verse 15 we find that the Son, Jesus Christ, is the image of the invisible God. In Greek, the word image (εικων) means likeness or image. The root of this word means "to appear". So we see here that Jesus is the image, likeness and appearance of the invisible God. This word is the same one used in the Septuagint (the Greek translation of the Old Testament) in Genesis 1:26 where God says *"Let us make man in our own image"*. So, while we find from Genesis that man was made *"in the image of God"*, we find from Colossians that Jesus Christ *"is the image of the invisible God"*. What a distinction!

This simple truth is in perfect agreement with the rest of Scripture, such as Hebrews 1:3, where the Holy Spirit says *"The Son is the radiance of God's glory and the exact representation of his being"*. The *"radiance of God's glory"* means that Jesus is the brightly-visible outward appearance of God's glory, the one that sheds God's light to all mankind. The *"exact representation of His being"*, is another clear statement revealing the truth that Jesus is not merely in the image of God, He is the image of God. He is exactly God's image, since He is the exact representation of His being. Amazing.

Returning to Colossians 1:15, we also find that Jesus is the firstborn of or over all creation. We note that this does not say that Jesus is the first of all creation, but that He is the firstborn of all creation. This statement identifies Jesus not as one part of creation but as one having inherited authority over it. This can be understood better in mortal-human terms by imagining a couple buying a piece of land for the purpose of building a home. They start by clearing the land and by building a foundation for the house. They continue by adding the structural members. They add plumbing, ventilation and electrical. They add on a porch, and they landscape the yard. They continue this building process step by step as they build their home. This particular couple is pregnant, and just as they are about to begin this building process they give birth to their son. He is their firstborn, and according to their custom he will inherit all that they have, including everything they are about to build. Anyone describing this couple and their homebuilding process could say that the foundation of the house was the <u>first</u> of their home, but they would have to declare that the son was the <u>firstborn</u> of their home.

Jesus Christ is the firstborn of all creation. What a position! What a responsibility. Yet at this point the Holy Spirit in Paul is just getting started. Let's see what other gems of truth we find in this passage.

As we continue in verse 16, we find that all things were created in or by Him (Jesus). Anyone familiar with the book of Genesis, will at this point think, "All things???" For from Genesis 1:1 we know that "*In the beginning <u>God</u> created the heavens and the earth*". Yet the Holy Spirit in Paul foresees this question and provides a resoundingly clear answer as He continues in verse

16, "*...things in heaven and on earth, visible and invisible, whether thrones or powers or rulers or authorities; all things have been created through him and for him.*"

Therefore, the Holy Spirit makes clear that Jesus Christ created all things, that is, all things in heaven and on earth. He extends and clarifies this statement by saying this includes things both visible and invisible. This means Jesus created all things both within our perception and outside of it.

Next, the Holy Spirit makes a very curious distinction extremely clear. He says "*...whether thrones or powers or rulers or authorities....*" We humans tend to imagine things, people, and animals when we consider creation. Yet here we find the Holy Spirit making a much more general and profound statement. He says that all beings, all authorities, all rulers, each and every being of power and prestige and position was created by Jesus Christ. This includes angels, cherubim, seraphim, living creatures of power, demons, and Satan himself. The Holy Spirit is saying that no authority or authoritative being exists that was not created by Jesus Christ. Wow. This is a statement beyond creation. It is a statement of Godhead. There is no authority outside of Christ that is not under Christ since all authorities were created by Him.

The Holy Spirit slams this point home as it concludes verse 16 with, "*...all things have been created through him and for him.*" At this point we see the whole picture. This statement also resolves our concern and questions that emanate from our understanding from Genesis that <u>God</u> created the world and everything in it. Verse 16 sets up this conflict and resolves it. All things were created by Jesus, through Jesus, and for Jesus. This is really deep truth, a huge gem lying on the surface of the Scripture, yet it lies right on top to be gleaned from the pages and tasted, enjoyed and digested. The statement that all things were made by Jesus shows that He did it. The statement that all things were made through Jesus shows that someone else created all things through him. This does not diminish the statement that Jesus created all things, it enhances and clarifies it. Jesus created all things, but he did not do it alone. Someone did it through Him, and shared in the creative event and process. This someone is identified in Genesis 1:1 as God Himself. The fact that God had company in this creative event is not new in the sense that it was not indicated previously in Scripture, yet it is new in the sense that it was obscured or hidden or left a bit of a mystery in times past, but has now been revealed. Let's take a look at this for just a moment.

In Genesis 1:1 Scripture says *"In the beginning God created the heavens and the earth"*. The Hebrew word used for God here is Elohim (אלהים). This word is actually plural. The singular word used for God in Scripture is either El (אל) or Eloha (אלוה), and both words are used to denote God or imagined gods throughout Scripture. Yet in Genesis 1:1 we find the plural form (Elohim) used to name our creator. We can imagine how this puzzled people studying Scripture throughout the centuries, since Scripture is so clear that there is only one God, and Scripture often expands this statement further to say that besides Him (God) there is no other (See Isaiah 44:8, 45:5-6, 45:18, 46:9 and elsewhere). Yet now we see the completed picture that there is no other who *apart from God* is God, yet there is Another who <u>as</u> a part of God <u>is</u> God. This person is Jesus Christ (the Word), who in the beginning was <u>with</u> God and who also <u>was</u> God as we saw in John 1:1. Therefore this use of the plural word for God reveals that there is a plurality in the Godhead, and this plurality points to the revelation that Jesus Christ is also God and shares in the Godhead.

In Genesis chapter 2 we find the creation event described again in summary fashion, and starting in verse 4 we find God named as Yahweh Elohim (יהוה אלהים). Here we again find the plural word for God (Elohim), and we see it coupled with His name (Yahweh), which means the existent one, the eternal one, and probably much, much more. Once again we see the plurality within God shrouded in mystery here, visible to the reader but not fully revealed and clarified as the Holy Spirit does in Colossians. It is curious here to note that God identifies Himself in this passage as Yahweh Elohim. This is generally translated "The Lord God" in English Bibles, and is generally viewed as another name of God. So we see here that Yahweh was present in creation. In Chapter 1 of Genesis his actions were included as part of the name Elohim, yet in Genesis 2 His role is separated and emphasized. Next we recall as we saw before that the name Elohim is the plural form of the word god, so when we see this name used here we expect it to include two or more persons within that name. Since Yahweh has been separately identified in this case, we see that at least two additional persons are included in the Godhead. We know from Colossians 1 that one of these persons is Jesus Christ, by, through, and for whom all things were created, and we see from Scripture elsewhere that the

Holy Spirit is the third person in this Godhead (See Psalm 51:11, Isaiah 63:10, Matt. 12:32, Matt. 28:19, Luke 3:22, 12:10, John 14:26, 15:26, Acts 5:32, 7:51, 13:2, 15:28, 21:11, Rom. 15:13, 15:16, I Cor. 6:19, Eph. 4:30, I Thess. 4:8, 2 Tim. 1:14, Titus 3:5, Heb. 3:7, 9:8, 10:15, I Peter 1:12).

Having seen from the opening words of Genesis that there is something about and within God that is more than the Single Being who was understood by mankind before Christ, we can now return to our passage in Colossians and be confident that what we find there is not something outside of the Scripture that was presented previously to mankind, but that we now have a revelation that is in perfect agreement with the first words that were spoken by the Holy Spirit to the heart and spirit of mankind.

Therefore, as God's Word in Colossians says, all things were created by Jesus, through Jesus, and for Jesus. We saw how things were created <u>by</u> and <u>through</u> Jesus. We now can consider that they were actually made <u>for</u> Jesus. Jesus is not merely the creator of all things, He is the one things were created for. As we begin to understand this simple truth, we begin to feel the overwhelming tragedy that exists since so many of us within mankind who were created by and through and for Jesus have sadly chosen to reject Him as Lord and Savior of our lives.

Let's return for a moment to our analogy of that couple who gave birth to their firstborn son just as they were on the brink of buying a piece of land and starting the process of building a home. Now let's imagine that father waiting until his son has grown a bit, and imagine that father laying that foundation and everything after it with his son. Let's say that the father decides not to lay one form, nor to raise one beam, nor to hammer one nail on his own, but that he instead chooses to patiently perform each action through his son. Let's imagine that the son is two years old at this point, and that this son lays each form, pounds each nail, and performs each detail of the build process. Our loving father holds the waist of his son, steadies his arm, and whispers each instruction into his son's ear. Our obedient son carefully follows the father's every command, moves with each slight suggestion of the father's hand, and adds his strength to his father's as they perform each action of the building process. The father's intent is to build a home, and to live in the home, but the father and the mother are in agreement that this home is being built by and through and for this beloved firstborn son of theirs.

When the work is complete it will be accurately stated that this home was built by and through and for the son. An observer could accurately state that the father built the house. He could state that the son built the house. He could state that they built it together. He could state that the father built it through the son. He could state that the father built it for the son. Each of these statements is true. This is what Colossians says. This is what Colossians reveals about the role of the Lord Jesus Christ in creation. Amazing.

Now that this is clear, we can continue with our passage in Colossians. We'll repeat it for clarity, starting in verse 17.

> *[17]He is before all things, and in him all things hold together. [18]And he is the head of the body, the church; he is the beginning and the firstborn from among the dead, so that in everything he might have the supremacy. [19]For God was pleased to have all his fullness dwell in him, [20]and through him to reconcile to himself all things, whether things on earth or things in heaven, by making peace through his blood, shed on the cross.*

"*He is before all things*". As we consider our home-building couple, it is obvious that they would describe their son as before all things. Christ is also before all things. He is before all things because he made all things. He is also before all things because He is more important. He is before all things because all things were made for Him. This statement is simple, elegant, and true.

"*In him all things hold together*". This is something new, yet it agrees perfectly with other Scripture, such as Hebrews 1:3, which states that Jesus (the Son) is "*sustaining all things by his powerful word*". Jesus holds all things together, and He sustains them by His powerful word.

In our home-building analogy, all things were made by, through, and for the son. Yet the son does not hold all things together in this analogy; the nails did, as did the cement, the glue, and so-forth. Yet here we find that Jesus Christ, the Son of God, holds all things together. He created all things and he also holds them together. All things are held together in Him. This is an enormous statement. This is a statement of Jesus' Godhead. As we come to understand that all things were made by and through Jesus and that all the things

He created include things in heaven and on earth, visible and invisible, including thrones, powers, rulers, and authorities, we realize that only God Himself can hold things this diverse, enormous, and powerful together. This reveals that Jesus Christ, who holds all things together, is God Himself. He is separate and distinct from but also a part of God the Father. God the Father works through and for Jesus, and the actions and image and person of these two are inseparable and can often be indistinguishable by mortal man. What beauty! What a concept! What a God!

Our passage continues in verse 18, *"And he is the head of the body, the church"*. Jesus is the head of the body. The body is the church. Jesus is the head of the body of believers.

"...and the firstborn from among the dead...." Jesus is the firstborn of God. He is also the firstborn from the dead. He conquered death on the cross (Rom 6:1-14, 23, 8:2, 2 Tim. 1:10, Heb. 2:14, Rev. 1:18). He raised Himself from the dead (John 2:19), and by doing so He conquered death for us. He is the first in resurrection and the firstborn of resurrection. Since He has conquered death and authored resurrection we can share in life with resurrection through Him. This is

what John 1 is pointing towards when is says that Jesus is life.

"...so that in everything he might have the supremacy." The Greek word translated supremacy here is pro-te-u-on (πρωτευων), which means first place, preeminence, or supremacy. This statement reveals the reason God created all things through His Son, the reason He created all things for Him, the reason He shares His Godhead with Jesus, the reason He has placed all things under Jesus' feet. God loves His Son (John 3:35, 5:20, 10:17, Col. 1:13), and He wants His Son to have supremacy over all things, so He has given supremacy over all things to His Son.

Let's continue with verse 19 of Colossians chapter 1.

> *19For God was pleased to have all his fullness dwell in him, 20and through him to reconcile to himself all things, whether things on earth or things in heaven, by making peace through his blood, shed on the cross.*

Jesus is the image of God, and all the fullness of God's deity dwells in Jesus. All of it. The reason the fullness of God's deity dwells in Jesus is because this pleases God. It was and is God's intent for His Son to have preeminence, or supremacy, or first place in everything. This is why He created all things by, through and for Jesus. This is why God created nothing and no-one outside of Jesus. This is why God allows Jesus to rule at His right hand. God is pleased for all of the fullness of His deity to dwell in Jesus Christ, and for Jesus to have first place in everything. He has also chosen for all reconciliation to be made through Jesus, and this reconciliation is made possible through the blood of Jesus, shed on the cross, which paid our debt of sin (Matt. 1:21, 26:28, Mark 2:10, Luke 5:24, Acts 2:38, 10:43, Rom. 3:21-26, 6:23, 7:24-25, 8:2-3, Gal. 1:4, Eph. 1:7, Col. 2:13, Heb. 9:15, 9:28, I Peter 2:24, 3:18, I John 1:7, 1:9, 2:2, 2:12, 3:6, 4:10, Rev. 1:5) and enabled Jesus to author resurrection for us.

This passage in Colossians paints a glorious picture of our God Yahweh authoring creation and life and everything we know, and doing it all through His Son Jesus Christ, so that His beloved little boy can BE GOD. As the seed and heir of God, Jesus is God, and as the one who actually performed all creation acts He is God, and as the One who paid our debt He is God, and as the One who conquered death, He is God.

This is why we are admonished in Colossians 2 to guard our thoughts and beliefs carefully, as we see starting in verse 8.

Jesus is the Source of Wisdom (Colossians 2:8-10)

Having laid a clear foundation for unveiling the beautiful mystery of the Godhead of Jesus Christ in chapter 1, the Holy Spirit now admonishes us through the apostle Paul to take care that our minds are not captivated by falsehood regarding Jesus Christ, as we see starting in verse 8 of chapter 2.

> *[8]See to it that no one takes you captive through hollow and deceptive philosophy, which depends on human tradition and the elemental spiritual forces of this world rather than on Christ. [9]For in Christ all the fullness of the Deity lives in bodily form, [10]and in Christ you have been brought to fullness. He is the head over every power and authority.*

In this passage the Holy Spirit, through Paul, warns us to beware of hollow and empty philosophy. The Greek word used here for philosophy is philo-so-fee-as (φιλοσοφιας) which literally means friend of wisdom, or one with affection towards wisdom.

Philosophy involves the study of things which cannot be perceived by the senses, including such things as reality, existence, knowledge, values, and reason. It relies on a systematic approach using rational arguments.

Pythagoras, who lived about 500 years before Christ, is said to be the first one to call himself a philosopher. He is greatly admired and respected for his contributions to philosophy and mathematics, yet he was also influential in the areas of religion and mysticism.

While those who practice philosophy concern themselves with the study and pursuit of wisdom, they do so in reliance on their own observational and rational abilities. The field of science today is also rooted in the observable, and in rational construction of ideas based on observations.

This is exactly the type of wisdom that the Holy Spirit is warning us against in Colossians 2:8. It says that philosophy depends on human tradition, and that it is hollow and deceptive. It says that this reliance on philosophy, which relies on rational thought and on human observations, does not remain untainted by outside influence, but that it also is affected by elemental spiritual forces of this world rather than by Christ. The elemental spiritual forces of this world that are not living in subjection to Christ today are demonic, and are intent on the destruction of mankind and of all things good and godly. Therefore, what this passage is warning us against is reliance on ourselves, on our own intellect, and on our own rational abilities. It is warning us that these abilities will lead us astray, and that these abilities are subject to malicious spiritual tampering.

Having warned us against reliance on ourselves, and against reliance on our own rational abilities, and against reliance on the knowledge of mankind, this passage points us back to the simple truth that Christ is the fullness of Deity in bodily form, that we are made complete in Him, and that He is the head over every power and authority. This includes our own power and authority, that of our wise men and philosophers, and that of demonic spiritual forces who seek to lead us astray.

This truth is in perfect agreement with the whole of Scripture, such as Psalm 111:10, Proverb 1:7, Proverb 9:10, Isaiah 11:3, and Isaiah 33:6, which each present facets of the truth that the fear of the Lord is the beginning of wisdom, knowledge, understanding, and instruction, in contrast to relying on our own powers of observation or on our own judgment.

This truth is also in perfect agreement with Colossians 1 and 2, which state so clearly that reliance on human wisdom will never result in a full understanding of spiritual things, which can only be accurately understood through reliance on the teaching and prodding of the Holy Spirit.

This truth is in stark contrast to the popular teaching and thinking of mankind today, which admires and seeks to emulate Pythagoras, Socrates, Plato, Darwin, and others like them, who through human reasoning or scientific observation have constructed elaborate beliefs about the beginning of things, about the world around us, about the history, achievements and goodness of mankind, and about God himself. This type of thinking can only lead us into error.

In contrast, those who seek to understand things, to find true wisdom, must submit all of their thoughts, abilities, intellect, observations, and conclusions to the Holy Spirit by bathing all these human faculties in the writings of Scripture, and by tempering all these faculties and abilities in the fires of what they find written there. Only in full surrender to the Spirit and to the Writings of God can a man or woman hope to find wisdom, knowledge, or an understanding of Spiritual things.

As it says in verse 9, it is in Christ Jesus that we are brought to fullness. He is the source, the beginning, the wellspring, of wisdom, knowledge, and understanding.

Jesus is the Source

Therefore, we find that the Son of God, Jesus, is the Source. He is the Source of creation, life, and light. He is the Source of our inheritance in the kingdom of light. He is the Source of creation. He is the Source of wisdom, knowledge and understanding. He is the wellspring of all things pertaining to godliness and goodness.

If we seek to reflect God to the world around us, then we must first understand that Jesus is the Source of all spiritual light and of all knowledge about God. Only after fully accepting this principle are we ready to examine our role in reflecting His light to the darkened world around us.

4

Light Lacker

We have now seen clearly that Jesus Christ is the source of life, light, salvation, and wisdom. We see that He is fully and completely God, the creator and sustainer of all things. We understand that light is the knowledge and understanding of God and of spiritual things, and that light is life, and that Jesus is the source of it.

Our goal in this book is to improve our ability to shine God's light on earth. To do this we must rely on the source of light, Jesus Christ, and learn to reflect His light to the world.

Unfortunately, we often fail to do this. The most common failing of mankind is the attempt to shine our own light on earth. We seek to shine knowledge and understanding and wisdom of both earthly and spiritual things to our fellow man through the use and exercise of our own faculties and giftedness and goodness. We seek to shine our own light, and we seek to add our light to that of Jesus Christ. Some of us even think deep down that the light we have to offer may be brighter than the one available to us through Jesus Christ as revealed through Scripture.

We do these things because we do not understand the completeness of Jesus as the source of light, and we do these things because we do not understand our own selves. We do these things because we understand neither what we are made from nor what we were made for.

We have already clearly demonstrated that Jesus is the source of light in the last chapter, so we can now turn our attention to understanding just who we are, what we are, what we were made for, and what we have to offer in regards to light and life.

We can begin to understand these concepts by simply researching what we are made from and what we were made for.

What We Are Made From

The first book of Scripture tells us clearly what we are made from. Genesis 2:7 tells us that the Lord God formed man from the dust (עפר) of the earth (האדמה). The Hebrew word for dust is aphar (עפר). If we examine all the places this word is used in Scripture, we find that it is used about 41 times in the context of the dust of the earth, about 36 times in contrasting the lowliness or humble state of mankind, about 11 times in the context of the grave or death, and about 7 times in the context of the numerousness or uncountability of something.

Therefore, we find that man is made from the dust of the earth. Note that we are not merely made from earth, we are made from the dust of it. It is hard to imagine a lower beginning state for mankind than the dust of the earth. If this concept is slow sinking in, go outside and grasp a handful of earth. Look closely at the clumpiness of it. It lies lifeless and lightless in your hand. Blow on it, and observe the dust of that earth scattering from the clump, into the wind, and out and down to the ground to lie indistinguishable from the mass of earth where it finds rest. This is what man was made of. Without God's creative action and love and life and purpose we are nothing but dust, which can be gathered without expense and cast away without consequence.

Having been made from the dust of the earth, we find that we (mankind) come from a most lowly or humble state. This is emphasized by the observation that the second most frequent use of the word aphar (עפר) in Scripture is used in a way that reminds us of this connection with dust and of our humble state. God proclaims this truth in Genesis 3:19, where He declares, *"...for dust you are, and to dust you shall return"*. Abraham admits it in Genesis 18:27, where he says, *"...for I am just dust and ashes"*.

We (mankind) want to believe that we are something special, that something good and alive and even godlike resides in us, that we have a purpose and that we can evolve from nothingness to somethingness just on our own merit and adaptation abilities. Yet this idea lies in direct contrast to the truth of Scripture, which reveals that without God's intervention, mankind is nothing but dust and ashes, lifeless and lightless and unable to emerge into anything without outside intervention.

Our lowly state, as well as our frailty and our short time here on earth, are also suggested in Scripture by the use of dust in the context of the grave or death. Passages such as Job 17:16, Job 21:26, and Psalm 22:15 present this aspect of the word, reminding us that we not only emerged from the dust of the earth, but that we shall also return there. Without God we clearly have no light, no life, no purpose.

What We Were Made For

Mankind on his own is truly a "light lacker", and could also be described as a "life lacker". Yet God's intervention gave us life, light, hope and a purpose. Let's look for a moment at Genesis 1:26 and following.

> ²⁶*Then God said, "Let us make mankind in our image (*בצלמנו*), in our likeness (*כדמותנו*), so that they may rule over the fish in the sea and the birds in the sky, over the livestock and all the wild animals, and over all the creatures that move along the ground." *²⁷*So God created mankind in his own image (*בצלמו*), in the image (*בצלם*) of God he created them; male (*זכר*) and female (*ונקבה*) he created them.*

Although God made mankind from the dust of the earth, which has no light, life, nor merit of its own, He fashioned us into His image, and into His likeness, which give us value and purpose and life and hope. In this image and likeness we are able to rule over the other earthly lifeforms of creation such as the fish and the birds and the livestock and wild animals. This reveals that mankind's value arises from our relation and connection with God. As mankind we are simply dust and ashes. As images of God Himself we have form and purpose. Our connection and interaction with God also give us life. This is revealed in Genesis 2:7 as follows.

> ⁷*Then the Lord God formed a man* (האדם) *from the dust* (עפר) *of the ground* (האדמה) *and breathed into his nostrils the breath* (נשמת) *of life, and the man became a living being* (לנפש חיה)*.*

Not only did God form us from the dust of the ground as Scripture reveals in Genesis 2:7, He made us in His image and likeness as it says in Genesis 1:26-27, and He breathed life into us as we see in Genesis 2:7. Mankind's image, and our likeness, and our purpose, and our life all emerge from God Himself.

Man was made from the dust of the ground, a lowliest of states, but we were made in God's image and with God's life and with God's purpose. Our life and light and purpose all come from God, but only after and through the continued understanding of our worth outside of Him and His continued action. This observation is consistent with the entirety of Scripture.

Although mankind is made from mere dust of the ground, we are made in the image of God. As we emulate His image, we have value and purpose. We bear His likeness, and we were made to bear His likeness. As we nourish and nurture His likeness within ourselves, we have value, and purpose, and we accomplish the purpose He created us for. We see this truth repeated throughout Scripture.

We see in John 1 that Jesus is the Light of God who became flesh and entered the world. In John 8:12, Jesus declares, *"I am the light of the world. Whoever follows me will never walk in darkness, but will have the light of life."* Jesus is the light of the world. All who follow Him experience His light, which enables them to see and to walk in light. Yet in John 9:5 Jesus says, *"While I am in the world, I am the light of the world."* Jesus says here that He is the light of the world as long as He is in the world. Yet one may wonder what happens next? Is Jesus still the light of the world after He leaves the world? If we follow Scripture further we find that in John 12:36 Jesus says, *"Believe in the light while you have the light, so that you may become children of light."* This means that as we believe in Jesus and walk in Him, we become children of light. Yet what does children of light mean? Does this merely mean that we walk in light, as we saw earlier, or does it imply more? Once again, Scripture unveils this truth further, as we see in Matthew 5:14, where Jesus declares:

> *[14]"You are the light of the world. A town built on a hill cannot be hidden. [15]Neither do people light a lamp and put it under a bowl. Instead they put it on its stand, and it gives light to everyone in the house. [16]In the same way, let your light shine before others, that they may see your good deeds and glorify your Father in heaven."*

Beautiful! Now we see the complete truth in all its glory. We are the light of the world. Our light is not in or of ourselves, it comes through Jesus. As we believe and walk in Jesus, we become children of Jesus, and since He is light, we become children of light. As children of light, we are able to see, and we are able to light the world. We do not shed our own light to the world, but we reflect the light of Jesus to it. We have no light of our own. We are merely the dust of the earth, but as the image of Jesus, as we emulate His light in our lives by reflecting His light, we walk in his likeness and therefore are able to share in His glory, and this glory is that we light the earth by reflecting Jesus' light to it.

Therefore we can see that Jesus is and was and will be the light of the world. For a time He shed His light directly on earth, yet now He has left that task to all who believe in Him and who walk in Him. Now that Jesus has returned to heaven He is still the light of the world, but the way He has chosen to light the world is through those of us who believe in Him and who reflect His light and who seek to emulate His image. What a task! If we do this poorly then the world develops a dim and distorted understanding of Jesus. If we do it well then the world is able to see clearly Jesus' beauty and love and salvation.

The apostle Paul understood this truth. In Acts 13 he and Barnabas were speaking in the synagogue in Pisidian Antioch, and the second time they spoke, the

Jewish leaders rejected them and their message due to jealousy. Acts 13:46+ records their response as follows:

> *[46]Then Paul and Barnabas answered them boldly: "We had to speak the word of God to you first. Since you reject it and do not consider yourselves worthy of eternal life, we now turn to the Gentiles. [47]For this is what the Lord has commanded us: "'I have made you a light for the Gentiles, that you may bring salvation to the ends of the earth." [48]When the Gentiles heard this, they were glad and honored the word of the Lord; and all who were appointed for eternal life believed.*

The Lord made Paul and Barnabas a light to the Gentiles. The light they shed was the message and ministry of Jesus. They were given a very special dispensation as apostles to the Gentiles, in the same way the other apostles were given one to minister to Jews. Yet we also share in this dispensation. In fact we who believe in Jesus and who follow Him share in the dispensation both to Jews and to Gentiles. This can be seen clearly in Matthew 28+ and elsewhere, where Jesus provides His final instructions to believers before returning to heaven.

¹⁸Then Jesus came to them and said, "All authority in heaven and on earth has been given to me. ¹⁹Therefore go and make disciples of all nations, baptizing them in the name of the Father and of the Son and of the Holy Spirit, ²⁰and teaching them to obey everything I have commanded you. And surely I am with you always, to the very end of the age."

This command from Jesus Himself commissions every believer to light the world (all nations) by making disciples of Jesus. As disciples of Him we emulate His actions and His message. As emulators of Him we reflect Him. As reflectors of Jesus we experience our role as "children of light" who "shine our light", yet the light we shed is not our own, it is that of Jesus Christ.

Mankind is made from the dust of the earth, and our bodies are returning to it. Yet we were made in the image and likeness of God to bear His image and likeness before mankind and before all creation. As bearers of His image we exercise dominion over the animal, bird and fish realms for the purposes of caring for our planet, yet more importantly we are to emulate Him by becoming more like Him in life, action, and message. As we emulate His life and proclaim His message we shed light to the earth, and this light is the knowledge and understanding and love of God through His Son Jesus Christ, the Savior and Redeemer of mankind. This is what we were made for: To become more like Jesus, and to proclaim His message to mankind.

Next we will look at how we can do this.

5

Righteous Reflector

We have now seen that the role and purpose of mankind is to shed the light of God to the world around us. This light of God is the understanding of Him, the knowledge of Him, and the love of Him. This light, knowledge, and love are all obtained through Jesus Christ, who God chose to elevate above all creation, authority, and power, due to His sonship, His obedience, and His connection with His Father, God Himself.

We have seen that we as mankind have nothing to offer in and/or of ourselves, since we are simply dust and ashes outside of God's creative and loving action. Yet we find that as believers in Jesus, and as followers of Him we have the ability and privilege to shine the light of God to the world around us by becoming children of light and by reflecting His light to those around us.

Yet how do we do this? How can we as mere dust reflect the light of God Himself when we have no light of our own?

In order to do this we must first understand that the source of Light is not ourselves, but is Jesus Himself, as we saw in Chapter 3. We must understand that we ourselves are lightless and that we have nothing to add to His light as we saw in Chapter 4, and we must understand how we can prepare ourselves to reflect the light of Jesus most fully to a dark and lightless world. As always, the key to understanding this task emerges from God's Word.

The Light of the World

Let's start by looking again at Matthew 5, starting in verse 14.

> [14]*"You are the light of the world. A town built on a hill cannot be hidden.* [15]*Neither do people light a lamp and put it under a bowl. Instead they put it on its stand, and it gives light to everyone in the house.* [16]*In the same way, let your light shine before others, that*

> *they may see your good deeds and glorify*
> *your Father in heaven."*

In this passage, Jesus calls us the light of the world. We saw previously that this light is not in or of ourselves but is simply a reflection of the light of Jesus Christ. We see here that we are not to horde the light we have been given, nor to hide it for our own secret enjoyment or use, but we are instead to place it in plain view for all to see and to benefit from.

Others may choose to hide from the light. They may dismiss it or try to construct structures that enable them to remain in darkness, but we are not to concern ourselves with that. We are simply to shed the light we have been given, or more accurately, to reflect the light that we can to those around us. In the same way that the moon hangs in the sky, reflecting the light of the sun, we who believe in Jesus and who follow Him are to reflect the light of Jesus to the world that looks upon our face. This is the task God has given us. This is the task Jesus commissioned His followers to fulfill.

Since we have been given this task, we must make every effort to prepare for it. Yet how do we do that? Let's look first at Ephesians 5, starting in verse 8.

⁸For you were once darkness, but now you are light in the Lord. Live as children of light. ⁹(for the fruit of the light consists in all goodness, righteousness and truth) ¹⁰and find out what pleases the Lord. ¹¹Have nothing to do with the fruitless deeds of darkness, but rather expose them. ¹²It is shameful even to mention what the disobedient do in secret. ¹³But everything exposed by the light becomes visible—and everything that is illuminated becomes a light. ¹⁴This is why it is said: "Wake up, sleeper, rise from the dead, and Christ will shine on you." ¹⁵Be very careful, then, how you live—not as unwise but as wise, ¹⁶making the most of every opportunity, because the days are evil.

We were in darkness when we were outside of the knowledge of Jesus and when we were not followers of Him. Yet now that we have this knowledge of Jesus Christ and this relationship with Him, we have become light and we are to live as light.

Jesus is the light, as we saw in John 1:4-9 and Colossians 1:12-13. We see here that the fruit of His light is all goodness, righteousness, and truth. This does not merely state that the fruit of Jesus' light is goodness, righteousness and truth, as if His fruit adds to our goodness, righteousness and truth. This states that the fruit of Jesus' light is <u>all</u> goodness, righteousness and truth. All of it. Outside of Jesus and His light there is no goodness, righteousness nor truth. These qualities are all a result of Jesus' light. Anything else that looks like goodness, righteousness or truth are simply cheap imitations that fall short of the fullness of the real qualities that are offered in and through Jesus Christ.

Having understood this truth, we are to emerge from darkness and pursue these qualities through Him. We do this by discovering what pleases Him, and by having nothing to do with the things that are opposed to His qualities of goodness, righteousness and truth.

Everything exposed to the light becomes visible. Everything that submits to being illuminated becomes light with us through Jesus. We are as good as dead in darkness, living in our dustness, and devoid of light and life. Yet when we become illuminated as Jesus' light shines on us, and when we submit to His light by enabling it to fill us and to change us, we awake from our sleep, we rise from the deadness of our dustness, and we become children of light, helping to illuminate the world around us.

This is what 1 Thessalonians is talking about in Chapter 5 where it says, *"⁵You are all children of the light and children of the day. We do not belong to the night or to the darkness."* Since we no longer belong to the night, nor to the darkness, we are to emerge from it and to bask in His light and in the fruit of it.

The world is full of darkness, and we were also full of it. Yet in and through Jesus we have become children of light, and as such we are to emerge from darkness and step into our role as children of light and as reflectors of Christ. We were in darkness, and it still fights to maintain a foothold in our lives, yet we must continue to strive to live in the light that Jesus supplies, and to let it fill our lives.

Emerging from Darkness (or Loving the Light)

Sadly, this is difficult for all of us. *John 3:19 says "This is the verdict: Light has come into the world, but people loved darkness instead of light because their deeds were evil."* How sad. Light has come, but many people have chosen to remain in darkness. Many, when exposed to light choose to scurry into deeper darkness, shunning the light and the penetrating exposure of their deeds that it supplies. Some revel in this, saluting darkness over light. Others pretend that darkness is light and light is darkness, living their darkened lives in the fantasy that deeds of darkness are good and deeds of light are evil. Yet perhaps the greatest tragedy is that many Christians also secretly admire certain aspects of darkness, and we tend to cultivate areas of our lives where we maintain a certain amount of darkness, so in the midst of our lightened lives we can return to the familiarity of darkness and strive to enjoy some aspect of the dark that we had known before. This often feels natural and good, since it is where we came from and it is where our old nature developed. Yet it is an empty place, without lasting satisfaction or fulfillment, and for those in Christ, visits to this area of our lives are often accompanied by a sense of doom or of foreboding, as the light of the Holy Spirit within us warns us of the danger and the corruption of the place.

Light and darkness are not compatible. Scripture states this repeatedly. Nature confirms it also, as the sun chases the darkness from one side of the world to the other and then back again. We can also see this principle in other realms. For example, developed countries typically understand the necessity to keep fresh and sewage water separate. They understand that if your bodily waste is stored too close to a fresh water source then the fresh water becomes contaminated and can carry sickness, disease and death. A small amount of waste can contaminate a large fresh water source, making it unfit for consumption. Deeds of darkness act in much the same way, and even a small amount can contaminate our lives so that the light of Jesus that we reflect becomes a darkened, contaminated version that does not appear at all the way He intended.

It is unfortunate that the light that many of us have in Jesus is just enough to illuminate the corruption in our own lives, making ourselves look like hypocrites and making Jesus look like a peddler of contaminated water. Yet if we cleanse ourselves of our darkened deeds, or more accurately, if we allow Jesus to wash through us and within us, then we can become clean enough for the light that He offers to reflect in a positive way to the world around us.

This is what 2 Corinthians 4:6 is talking about where it says:

⁶For God, who said, "Let light shine out of darkness," made his light shine in our hearts to give us the light of the knowledge of God's glory displayed in the face of Christ.

We who follow Christ will often feel like hypocrites, because we are of the darkness and have become children of light. As children of light we shine a light that is not our own to a darkened world. Yet as shiners of Jesus' light we find that we are heirs and partakers of Jesus, and that the light is our own since Jesus is ours and since He makes His light ours if we are willing to fully surrender to Him and to become reflectors of Him. The passage above says we are to let our light shine out of darkness. That darkness is the darkness of the world, and it is the darkness of our lives that we had, and of the darkness that strives to redarken our lives. Yet we are not to concern ourselves with that. As children of light, and as followers of Christ, we are simply to let light shine out of darkness. The way we do this is by letting His light shine in our hearts, His face shining off our face, so that the world can see the light and the life of Jesus reflecting off of us and penetrating through us.

As we act as reflectors of Christ, the world will get the light of Christ through us. As they look to and at us to see the light of Christ they will often see the remnants of darkness in our own lives, revealing us as the creatures of darkness that we were. Yet this is not to inhibit our role as reflectors, nor to undermine our determination to reflect the light He offers through our imperfect lives. Our role is simply to light the world by reflecting Jesus, and at the same time to submit to His cleansing and His cleaning of our lives, so that we become better vessels, better reflectors, better illuminators of the world and of ourselves through the light of Jesus Christ.

What an honor and a privilege this is! What a risk Jesus takes to allow us to be His face to the world! Yet Jesus loves us very much, and He wants us to share in the joy of becoming His face to the world. We should not ever feel shame to assume this wonderful role He offers us. We should relish the joy of becoming His face by reflecting His light, and as we do so we should also strive to become better reflectors of Him by becoming more like Him by extracting each deed and remnant of darkness from our lives.

Visible, Undistorted Light

As we understand that we are the light of the world as we reflect Jesus Christ, and as we begin to emerge from the darkness of the world and to expunge the darkness from within our own lives, then we are ready for the next truth, which Jesus' gave to the crowds as recorded in Luke 11. We will pick up His thoughts in verse 33.

> [33]*"No one lights a lamp and puts it in a place where it will be hidden, or under a bowl. Instead they put it on its stand, so that those who come in may see the light."*

In this passage, Jesus is reminding us that we must be visible. Our duty is to reflect His light. As we do this we become lights, or lamps, as we effectively shine His light as it reflects off of our lives. We cannot let the corruption of the world, or our fear of repercussions, or our shame at our own hypocrisy, or anything else stand in the way of our role as lamps and lights as we reflect Christ.

It is hard to understand why Jesus chose to take this great risk by allowing us to take any part in reflecting His light to the world. Yet He has. He loves us very much, and in the same way that a father takes pleasure when his little son or daughter imitates him, Jesus takes pleasure when we imitate Him by reflecting His light and by sharing His Word to those around us.

Jesus has chosen to entrust us with the responsibility of reflecting His light to mankind. In fact, many on earth know nothing of Christ except what is reflected from the few Christians with whom they interface. It is sad that so many of us do a poor job of reflecting His light without distorting it. Yet Jesus took this risk by entrusting us with this role of reflecting His light.

Imagine a man falling in love with a beautiful woman. He is a good man, with a fine income, and a compassionate heart, and he longs to make himself and his love known to this woman. Yet instead of revealing himself and his love to her directly, he instead chooses a trusted friend and entrusts his message of love to this friend. He entreats his friend to show this woman the kind of man that he is, and he entrusts him with his very words of love and with his proposal of marriage, and in doing so he jeopardizes everything. Everything he is, everything he feels, everything he promises is now at risk, because all the woman will ever know of the man is what is related through his friend. He is at risk of the friend not accurately relaying his message. He is at risk of the friend leaving out some critical detail. He is at risk of the friend placing the wrong emphasis or of him adding something. He is at risk of the friend deliberately distorting the message for his own purposes. He is at risk that the friend's life will not accurately reflect his own, since the woman will probably carefully evaluate the kind of man the friend is and will estimate that the man is some similar sort of person. A man in love would only entrust such a message to a friend he dearly loves, and to one he trusts implicitly.

Yet Jesus entrusts us with His message. He loves us implicitly, yet He knows and we know that we are not worthy of His trust. We distort His message. We change the emphasis based on our own desires and preferences. We shirk our responsibility and often only share little tidbits of His message.

Perhaps this is why Jesus continues in this passage to provide a warning. Let's pick up His message again in verse 34 of Luke 11.

> [34]*"Your eye is the lamp of your body. When*
> *your eyes are healthy, your whole body also*
> *is full of light. But when they are unhealthy,*
> *your body also is full of darkness.* [35]*See to*
> *it, then, that the light within you is not*
> *darkness."*

We know that we are lamps as we reflect Jesus' light. Yet here Jesus brings a new principle to our attention. Here He informs us that our eye is the lamp of our body. Since we know that we are not lamps outside of our role as reflectors of His light, this means that our eye is the key to our ability to reflect His light. This means that what we can see and understand will affect our ability to reflect His light.

Jesus says that when our eyes are healthy, our whole body is full of light, and when our eye is unhealthy, our body is full of darkness. This means when we can see and perceive well, we will be filled with light, and when we cannot, we will be filled with darkness. The thing we must be able to see and perceive and understand is Jesus Himself. We see Him and perceive His intentions, and understand His ways and His message as we study His Word. If our eye is healthy, then we see accurately, we understand correctly, and we perceive His intentions rightly, and the result of this healthy ability to see and understand His Word and ways enables us to be fully filled with light, such that we can reflect this light and shine it upon those around us.

Yet if our eye is unhealthy, then what we see and understand and perceive and imagine about Jesus Christ is distorted, and instead of filling us with light, this unhealthy perception fills us with darkness. When our eye is unhealthy because we are not able or willing to understand what Jesus intended through His Word and His Spirit, then we become like stained glass windows, distorting the light that enters us, darkening it, distorting it, and reflecting that perversion to the world around us. When this happens we become like those mirrors at the carnival that distort everything they reflect. When the world looks at itself in a carnival mirror, the skinny look fat, the fat look skinny, the straight look crooked, and anything beautiful appears like a monstrosity. When Christians do not have healthy eyes, then the reflection of Jesus that they provide is so distorted and ugly that the world looks on it in disgust and horror. What a tragedy that so many of us reflect Christ so poorly.

Yet there is hope. Jesus has not given up on us. He admonishes us to develop healthy eyesight. We do this by immersing ourselves in His Word, by surrendering fully to what we find there, by building each thought and reason from this source of truth. As we do this our eyes become healthier and healthier. As our eyes become healthy our mirror straightens, the glass inside us becomes clearer, and the light we shine is a more accurate reflection of His person and of His love.

This is the goal He points to in verse 36 of Luke 11.

> [36]*"Therefore, if your whole body is full of light, and no part of it dark, it will be just as full of light as when a lamp shines its light on you."*

When our eye is healthy because we see and understand Christ, then our whole body fills with light, and this light is undarkened and undistorted. When this happens we become full of light as if a lamp were shining on us, and a lamp is shining on us, and that lamp is Jesus Christ. Jesus is the Light, and the Lamp, and as He shines on us we become full of light and reflect this light upon mankind, and as we do this the world sees Him through us.

As the world sees Him through us some will come to Him. Their eyes will begin to grow healthy, and as they do they will fill with light, and will also reflect Jesus directly upon those around them.

What a privilege to be a part of the Jesus plan for lighting the world, for spreading the knowledge of Him, for sharing His message of love and devotion to the care of their souls.

The Coming Darkness

In Mark 13, Jesus warns His disciples about the end times. He says that as the end draws near, many will pretend to be Christ. He says that there will be earthquakes, wars, famine, and persecution. He says many will be deceived. Then He says something peculiar. In Mark 13:24 He says... *"But in those days, following that distress, the sun will be darkened, and the moon will not give its light"*. Many understand this to mean that the sun will actually be darkened and that the moon will actually appear dark, and I agree that Jesus meant this, since Isaiah 13:10, Revelation 6:12

and 8:12 all prophesy the same occurrence. However, our study of our role as light suggests that Jesus may have been prophesying something else as well. It may be that in the end times, Jesus will no longer allow Himself to be visible to the world, and the Christians here may no longer reflect His light to mankind. What a tragedy for those who still have not yielded to His love and plan for salvation, for they may lose their opportunity to see and to understand and to be saved.

Yet today we still have the light. Jesus is visible to mankind through Scripture, through recorded history, and through nature that proclaims His work. Christians still reflect His light, sharing His Word, emulating His works, and offering His love. Followers of Jesus have proclaimed His salvation throughout the world. Today there is no excuse for rejecting Jesus' love, and today we have the unique privilege of reflecting His face to mankind. Let us faithfully continue to strive to reflect Him well.

Summary

So, we see that the Son is the Source of Light. We lack light completely, yet we can provide light by reflecting Jesus Christ to mankind. We can improve our ability to shed Jesus' light by studying His Word and by conforming our thoughts and actions to all that is written there, and as we do this we can provide brighter, purer, less-distorted light to those with whom we come in contact.

Next we will look at how to position ourselves better, so that our light is more apparent and more effective to the world around us.

6

Perfect Positioning

When we look at the moon, we find that the amount of light that it reflects to earth varies as it traverses its path about the earth. It is curious to note that the moon always faces the earth with the same side. As it travels about the earth, this face gets aligned either increasingly or decreasingly toward the sun. The more the moon faces the sun, the more of the sun's light is able to reflect off of the moon's face towards earth. The less the moon faces the sun, the less of the sun's light reaches its face. Since the moon always faces the earth completely as it orbits the earth, this means that the moon's phases result from its face turning increasingly or decreasingly towards the sun. This means that the amount of light that the moon reflects to earth is a direct function of its position, and its position reveals how much the moon faces the sun at any given moment. This curious fact of nature unveils some deep insights for Christians.

New Moon Positioning

The new moon is so-called when the moon is directly in line with the sun. This means that it is between the earth and the sun. In this position, it completely faces the earth, and does not face the sun at all. This means that the sun's light is unable to reach any of the moon's face, such that the moon reflects no light to earth. In this position, the moon is also able to block the earth's view of the sun either partially or completely, depending on the time of year and the corresponding relative positions of earth and moon. Therefore, when the moon is new, observers on earth receive none of the sun's light reflected off its face, and at times they are also unable to see the sun itself since the moon is in the way. We call those times when the moon completely blocks the sun's light a solar eclipse.

As Christians, we can learn a valuable lesson from the effect of the positioning of the moon when it is in this phase. Just as the moon reflects none of the sun's light when it is completely facing earth and has its back to the sun, in the same way Christians, when we turn our faces away from Christ and towards the world, we become unable to see God's will for us, we shed none of His light to mankind, and we also obscure mankind's view of God Himself.

Many of us experience phases in our lives, just as the moon does. We experience times of facing Jesus completely. We experience times of turning partially or completely from Him, and focus instead on our own lives, our own desires, our own passions. Yet whenever we turn completely from Jesus and focus solely on worldly things, our light vanishes, we appear dark to those around us, and we often obscure the view of those around us so that they cannot see Jesus either.

It is sobering to reflect upon our lives and to recognize all the times we have done this. It is saddening to think of the negative effect these periods in our lives have had upon our neighbors, our friends, acquaintances and loved ones. Yet we must press on. We must turn our faces back towards Christ, confess our sins, request Jesus' cleansing and renewal, and return to a position where we can reflect Christ more fully.

We must then take steps to guard ourselves from turning our faces again from Jesus, so that we can reflect His light, and maintain our role of light-reflectors towards mankind.

Full Moon Positioning

The moon is full when its position is opposite that of the sun in relation to earth. This means that the earth is between the moon and the sun. In this position, the moon completely faces the earth, and it also completely faces the sun. In this position it is able to present its full face to both earth and sun, such that the sun's light reflects off the entire face of the moon, and such that all of this light is reflected straight to earth to illuminate it. Therefore, when the moon is full, it is able to reflect the sun's light to earth to its full capacity, because it fully faces earth and it also presents its full face to the sun.

In the same way, when we as Christians fully face Jesus while maintaining our natural lives here on earth, we are able to reflect Him fully to those around us. Obviously, the light we reflect is nothing compared to His direct light, but it is the maximum light that we can reflect for the current state of our reflective properties, which include the depth of our knowledge of Him through Scripture, our submission to the Holy

Spirit, the purity of our lives, and the net effects of our past choices and of our spiritual successes and failures.

Other Moon Phase Positioning

The moon is bound to orbit the earth in an endless cycle where it moves from new moon to full moon and back again. As it orbits the earth, its position enables it to present ever-increasing amounts of its face to the sun as it moves from new moon to full moon positions, and ever-decreasing amounts of its face as it moves from full moon to new moon positions. The result of these changes of position is that either more or less of the sun's light gets reflected to earth as either more or less of the moon's face is presented to the sun.

In the same way, our success in facing Christ will ebb and wane throughout the course of our lives. Our track record in facing Him fully is affected by our interests, our work, our friends, family, and events around us. We must never lose heart in continually seeking Him, so that our faces can reflect His light to those around us.

Christian Positioning

We have seen that we who dwell here on earth are much like the moon in that our face is always towards earth. We cannot help but face earth since we are here and must function, survive, and thrive. Yet those of us who worship and serve God through His Son Jesus Christ also have eyes that seek Him as well.

Our eyes look to earth but they also look towards Jesus Christ, our Savior and Redeemer. As events in our life unfold about us, our eyes look increasingly or decreasingly towards Jesus, yet they remain steadfastly fixed towards earth. As we progress through life we constantly face earth and those around us, but we also face towards Jesus in larger or smaller amounts.

Just as the moon orbits the earth, ever facing her, and presents increasing then decreasing amounts of its face to the sun, in the same way we face earth constantly, and we also present our face towards Jesus in increasing or decreasing amounts. When our eyes are completely fixed on Christ, our face is able to reflect Jesus' full light to earth. As our face turns from Christ, we are able to reflect less of His light to those about us. At times, we turn our faces completely from

Christ and present our backs to Him. In this position, we are unable to reflect any of His light, and we also tend to block the view of others around us such that they cannot see Him at all.

Regardless of position, the intensity of the light we reflect will be a function of the kind of reflectors we have become. If our lives are pure, and we are immersed in His Word, and we are growing in our faith and allowing it to fill us and to change us as we conform to the image of Christ, then the intensity of the light we reflect will be great. As we let sin take hold and fester in our lives, then the reflective properties of our lives will be damaged and we will reflect less of Jesus' light, or we will reflect a distorted version of it.

The quality of our reflective properties in life will tend to vary as we succeed or fail in increasing or decreasing amounts. Our goal should be to ever-grow in His image, yet unfortunately we often fall short of the mark and find ourselves slipping backward at times along the way.

Meanwhile, as we struggle to conform to His image such that we reflect Christ ever-brightly, the amount of light we reflect is also a function of whether our faces are fully turned to Him. The more we face Christ, the more of His light we reflect. As our lives are pure and conformed to His purpose and will, this light will be intense, clean, bright, and will accurately present His image to mankind. The less we face Him, the less of His light will be reflected. The less we are conformed to his image, the dimmer the light will be that we reflect, and the more distorted a picture of Him that those about us will see from us.

So we find that our role in lighting the earth has two specific influences, a short term influence and a long-term one.

The short-term influence is our positioning. Our positioning is really a function of which way we face, or where we set our eyes. When we set our eyes towards Christ it is like reflecting His full light. When our eyes are fully on Him, we present the most of His image to those around us. As our eyes turn from Him, we reflect less of His light, to the point of reflecting none at all whenever we take our eyes off of His.

The long-term influence is the quality of our reflector. Our reflector is really the righteousness of our lives. As our lives conform to Jesus image we become like great reflectors, and our lives reflect His image brightly and accurately. As our lives deform from Jesus' image, we become like poor reflectors, or like carnival mirrors, that dim or distort Jesus' image to mankind.

The collective effectiveness of our ministry in life is a function of both our position and our reflective properties.

Our reflective properties take time to develop. Our righteousness only springs from Christ Himself. We must immerse ourselves in His Word, understand it, live and breathe it, allow it to penetrate and change each aspect of our lives. This takes time. As we focus on this we slowly become better and better reflectors of His image as we conform to it.

Our position can be changed immediately. At any moment we can turn our eyes to Jesus, look full on His face, and present as much of ourselves to Him for His immediate use. When we do this, we present our full faces for the use of reflecting Christ. As the full moon presents its entire face for reflecting the sun's light, when we take a full-moon position we present our full face to Jesus and allow Him to reflect off of what we are to mankind around us. This is risky business. It is risky for us and it is riskier for Jesus. This is because when we reflect Jesus completely, our lives are the reflector, and whatever we are also becomes apparent to those around us. As we reflect Christ our sin and hypocrisy and shortcomings all come into full view of the world. These defects in us darken the light we reflect and distort it. This is risky for us.

This is riskier for Christ because He is perfect. Why would He enable us in our deformed and corrupted state to so effectively distort His beautiful attributes to the world? It is hard to fathom why Jesus would take such a risk. Yet He does. He loves us so much that He takes this risk with us. As a father loves His son or daughter, and delights in their attempts to emulate him, in the same way Jesus loves us, and encourages us to grow in Him by assuming His role as light when we are willing to reflect Him.

Therefore, we have a duty here on earth, and this duty involves two determined, intertwining actions on our part. Our duty is to reflect Christ. This is our duty and our privilege. To do so we must first set our eyes on Him, presenting our full face to Him and letting it reflect Him unhindered. Then we must conform ourselves to His image, and keep on striving to do so. Whenever we find our eyes have drifted from His face to view things on earth instead, we need to reset our eyes back to His. Whenever we find our lives have drifted from conformity to His image we must strive to bring it back in line. Yet we should never stop presenting our full face to Christ simply because our lives have drifted into nonconformity with His image. We should also never stop trying to conform to His image simply because our eyes have looked away.

The first step is always to look back to Christ. The second is to work on conforming to His image so He can restore and replenish righteousness within us. As our lives ebb and wane our success will often do the same. Yet we must ever-look to Him. We must boldly reflect His image off of our world-stained lives, and we must ever-strive to conform to His will and ways.

This will please our Lord. This will light this world. What an honor to be a part of God's redemptive plan.

7

Closing Comments

The moon is a great reminder to us of our role and responsibility in this life. The moon's role in reflecting the sun's light bears a striking similarity to the role of the Christian to reflect Jesus to the people around us.

Jesus is the source of light, life, and salvation for mankind. There is no substitute for His light, nor any additive that can enhance His light.

As we grow in understanding the perfection of His being as our source of light, we are reminded of how lacking we are in our ability to add anything to His light. As we understand this truth, we realize that the only way to shed light on earth is to strive to bring our person and position into line with His will and Word. We bring our person into line by immersing ourselves in God's Word and by letting the Holy Spirit to change us into His image. This donning of Christ is like dressing in His clothes, yet it is more, because we are not merely wearing His clothing, we are changing our skin and person into a likeness of Him. This is righteousness, not being righteous in or of ourselves, but having His righteousness placed over, on, and through us, such that it cleanses us and we become more like him. In this way we become righteous reflectors of Christ.

As we don Christ, such that our lives better reflect His beauty and perfection, we also keep our eyes on Him, and strive to allow nothing to get between us and His Will or Word. As we keep our faces full towards Christ, our lives become more-fully visible and evident to those around us, allowing us to reflect Christ fully.

As the moon is made of material perfectly suited for reflecting the sun's light, our lives become material perfectly suited for reflecting Christ.

As the moon reflects more of the suns light as it faces earth without allowing the world to block its view of the sun, our lives reflect more of Christ when we keep our faces full on His, and do not allow ourselves to turn away, nor allow the earth to block our view of Jesus.

In this way, we have the opportunity and privilege to participate with Christ in lighting this fallen world. What a gift. What a responsibility. What a challenge. What a task.

May the Lord bless you as you strive to become a better reflector of Jesus Christ, and as you strive to become and to remain perfectly positioned, so that Christ reflects fully off of your life and on to those around you.

A Poem

The following poem was written to my grandmother, Marjorie June Coburn, the day before her eighty-fifth birthday, long before this book was conceptualized in my mind. It is included here as a tribute to her.

<u>Reflection of His Son</u>

A quiet smile and spirit
Are the traits that mark this one
With her gentle wisdom whispered
'Neath an attitude of fun.

She's always quick to share a Scripture
In her kind and loving way,
And her blessing hits the mark
And often brightens up our day.

What a treasure to her family
And a source of warmth and joy.
What a teacher, friend and mentor
For her family to enjoy.

She's the Matriarch of Coburns
And she is known from East to West
As the mother of the seven
And the grandma of the rest.

And now tomorrow marks her birthday
Her eighty-fifth to be precise.
And what a special joy to celebrate
The birth of one so nice.

And so we lift our voice in praises
To the God who made this one
And we thank Him for this beauty,
This reflection of His Son.

Todd Coburn
December 18, 2005

About the Cover Photographer

Wally Pacholka, accountant by profession and astronomer by avocation, now specializes in capturing spectacular photographs of the night sky in national parks and wilderness areas of the United States. His work has been published in Time Magazine, Life Magazine, National Geographic, and elsewhere. His other spectacular photographs can be viewed and purchased online at Astropics.com.